The ghosts

Weymer Jay Mills

Alpha Editions

This edition published in 2021

ISBN : 9789355893895

Design and Setting By
Alpha Editions
www.alphaedis.com
Email - info@alphaedis.com

Contents

CHAPTER ONE

There was a clanging, brassy melody upon the air. For three-score years since York of the Scarlet Coats died, and the tune "God Save the King" floated for the last time out of tavern door and mansion window, the bells of old St. Paul's had begun their ringing like this:

"Loud and full voiced at eight o'clock sends good cheer abroad," said the tottering sexton. "Softer and softer, as folks turn into bed, and faint and sweet at midnight, when our dear Lord rises with the dawn." Cheery bells full of hope—gentle chimes, as if the holy mother were dreaming of her babe. Joyous, jingling, jangling bells! Through the town their tones drifted, over the thousands of slate-colored roofs, now insistent on the Broadway, now lessening a little in some long winding alley, and then finally dying away on the bare Lispenard Meadows.

Vesey Street—the gentry street—heard them first. The bigwigs in the long ago, with the help of Gracious George, built the church, and who had a better right than their children to its voices. Calm and serene lay Vesey Street with its rows of leafing elms. Over the dim confusion of architectural forms slipped the moonlight in silver ribbons, seeming to make sport of the grave, smug faces of the antiquated domiciles. Like a line of deserted dowagers waiting for some recalcitrant Sir Roger de Coverley, they stood scowling at one another. No longer linkboys and running footmen stuck brave lights into the well-painted extinguishers at each doorstep. No longer fashion fluttered to their gates. The gallants who had been wont to pass them with, "Lud! what a pretty house!" were most of them asleep now on the green breast of mother England, forgetful of that wide thoroughfare, which had never reckoned life without them.

Into the parlor of Knickerbocker House, dubbed Knickerbocker Mansion some years after the bibulous Sir William Howe had laid down his sceptre as ruler of the town, the chorus of bells crashed.

"What a dastardly noise!" cried Jonathan Knickerbocker, throwing his newspaper over his head. "Can this Easter time never be kept without an infernal bell bombilation? I shall call a meeting of the vestry—that idiot Jenkins should be kept at home!" The head of the Knickerbocker family turned irately in his chair and glared at his daughters. Three timid pairs of blinking eyes were raised from short sacks in answer to his challenge, then lowered again over the wool. The fourth and fairest daughter of the house, seated on the walnut sofa in the bow-window, gave no heed to his vehemence but a suppressed sigh. With a final snort the *Gazette* was picked up again. The Easter melody was waning.

The Knickerbocker parlor—not the state parlor, which had long been closed—was a dismal place—so large that four candles and one Rumford lamp made but a patch of brightness in the gloom. Most of the furniture was ponderous and ugly, with two or three alien little chairs that looked as if they might once have belonged to some light-hearted lover of the Louis. On the almost barren chimney-piece stood a pair of tall nankeen beakers, sepulchrally reminiscent of buried Chinese years. Along the walls hung a score of mediocre portraits, the handiwork of the usurious limner John Watson and his compatriot Hessilius. Spans of sunlit days had stolen every tinge of carmine from their immobile and woodeny faces, leaving them the drab color of time, in keeping with the room.

Above the cornice, near the sofa where Patricia Knickerbocker sat, hung an empty frame. The portrait it contained had been banished to the attic while her three eldest sisters were still in Wellington pantalets.

"The woman looks like a Jezebel," Jonathan had sputtered. "Och! that leering smile." He tried to blot from his mind the stray leaves he knew of her story, and the disturbing thought that she was of his blood. "She shall not remain with the likenesses of my ancestors!" he had told his sisters, who were over from Goby House.

When this descendant of the Knickerbockers spoke of his progenitors he always held his head a trifle more erect, and puffed out his pompous figure, though, strange to relate, like many another worthy man of a later day having the same foible, he knew very little about them. Of course he could have told you that the lady over the east bookcase, wearing a blue tucker and holding a spray of milk-weed in her hand, was his Aunt Jane; and that his father was a noted New York judge, the pride of three circuits. Or if his digression were extended, there was his trump card, one of the first American Knickerbockers, labelled "The Friend of Lord Cornbury!" These were the firmest rocks in his family history, to which he could climb in safety, thence to look down with scorn on those unfortunates beneath his social eminence. He was a Knickerbocker, of Knickerbocker Mansion, Vesey Street, and a member of one of the oldest families in York and America.

Patricia, smiling little Patricia, rummaging one day among the dust-bins under the eaves, had found the banished portrait. Juma, the gray-wooled negro, a comparatively new member of the Knickerbocker household, who had appointed himself her body-servant ever since his arrival at the mansion, was with her.

A faithful slave to old Miss Johnstone of Crown Street, Juma had been forced by his mistress's death into new service. He was a picture of ebonized urbanity, a good specimen of the vanished race of Gotham blacks, gentler in manners and clearer in speech than their Southern cousins. In his youth he had been sent to one Jean Toussaint of Elizabethtown to learn the art of hair-dressing. He could impart much knowledge of wigs to a wigless age, and talked in a grandiloquent fashion of Spencers, Albemarles, and Lavants. Many a beau peruke and macaroni toupee his lithe fingers curled and sprinkled with sweet flower-water. The voices of the fine people who were his visitors made constant music in his memory, and his tongue was ever ready with anecdotes of wizened beauties and uncrowned cavaliers.

Juma was faithful to the period of his greatest splendor. Deep in his heart he despised the home to which freedom and poverty had led him after the demise of his protectress. "Gold braid on company coat and silk stockings done ravel out in dese days. Knickerbockers talk quality, but dey ain't got quality mannahs—Missy Patsy is de only one of dem with tone."

He loved to listen to the girl as she tripped through the great rooms, humming softly some air from Lennet's "London Song-Book"—one of the relics of his "ole Miss." Patricia always sang on the days when her sisters were visiting their aunts on the bluff. Juma loved her, and during his five years' residence in the family had many times taken her youthful mind in train with quaint eighteenth-century maxims and fetiches.

"De wise miss drop her fan when she enters de ballroom," he would say. "Den she gets de men on der knees from de start."

"I wish I were invited to balls," Patricia sighed. "The Kings and Grahams give one or two every year, but father never notices them."

"Well, you jes' know how to behave," he chuckled. "Doan' yo' forget de tricks your Uncle Juma taught yo'."

When the two had met in the attic that April day, Juma's spirits were as ebullient as usual.

"How lovely she is, Juma! See, there is a blush on each cheek. Her pink brocade makes me think of a rose dancing in the wind."

Patricia stared into the canvas face before her and the lips seemed to curve themselves into the shadow of a smile. "I know you were the fairest one of us," she whispered, "the fairest and the best."

"Dat's the real quality way of holding the head," vouchsafed Juma. "I'se pow'ful 'clined to think she looks like yo', missy." And then they had laughed, shut away with maimed chairs, tired spinets, and other voiceless things, glad to have escaped from Knickerbocker frowns.

"How lovely she is, Juma!"

It was a dismal household, that of the old mansion—the master absorbed in his passion for wealth and worship of family; the three eldest daughters, who might once have had some individuality but now were moulded in the form of their father. "Callow old maids," any individual of the lower ranks of York would have dubbed them. They wore little bunches of sedate curls over each ear, and dressed in sombre, genteel colors proper to their exalted rank. On the first day of the week they dozed through a long sermon; on its last day they simpered politely at the Whist Club. Fears of broken jelly-moulds or of the romping Patricia's next prank were the only disturbers of the tranquillity of their lives. Jonathan Knickerbocker was their one Almighty Mirror. When he labelled Mrs. Scruggins, the draper's niece, a person not fit to associate with, their stiff gowns obediently gave forth hisses at the said lady. When he prated of his father's shrewdness, they nodded discreet approval; and at the mere mention of the loyal friend of Lord Cornbury, they bobbed like grass before a gale.

Patricia's impressionable temperament was saved by Juma's advent from the sirocco of dulness that wafted her sisters over the lake of years. His "ole Miss," a looker on at the "Court of Florizel," had unconsciously taught him to imbibe the atmosphere surrounding the Graces. A democracy could not spoil her elegance, for Chesterfield's warning was ever before her eyes. She who copied the footsteps of Baccelli, adored her Sterne and Beattie, and though her eyes grew dim, never let romance pass her window unmolested, had left her impress upon the mind of the faithful servitor. Life to him was a gay-colored picture-book, brighter perhaps because he could not read the printed page. All his maids were cherry-ribboned and belaced; all his roystering sparks clinked gilded canakins. Love was ever smiling on them! For wellnigh half a century he had listened to tales of the gay god as he bound one romance-loving woman's silken tresses. Small wonder that he thought the urchin ruled the world!

When the bells rested their brassy throats for the first time that night, and Jonathan Knickerbocker could take up his West Indies accounts undisturbed, giving his daughters freedom to doze in peace, "Miss Patsy" stole on tiptoe from the room. She wanted to be alone. Juma, ambling through the dim hall to his pantry, caught sight of her fluttering garments, but did not speak. Only an hour or two before, he had placed in the chamber where she slept a bunch of arbutus which young Sheridan, the organist, had given into his keeping. The wild, sweet-scented flower grew in but one spot near the town—an island in the centre of the Woodbridge Swamp, where Captain Kidd in a freak of fancy had planted it over the body of a comrade, tradition said, and no one ever disputed the story. To reach it, even the most sure-footed ran the danger of being caught in the bog.

Patricia wondered as she mounted the stairs how her lover had been able to come with her gift unseen. The watching negro smiled sadly and shook his head when the last bit of her garment disappeared over the staircase like a white moth moving treeward.

Oh, how terrible it was never to see him in her father's house! Never to have seen him alone, only that one time, after twilight service, when she had stolen a meeting at the Battery, while her family were taking their Sabbath-day ride up the Bowery Road!

The old vehicle held but six, and as the aunts always rode home with their brother, Patricia was left to the escort of Juma, custodian of the prayer-books. By the clump of protecting boxwood at the end of the Marine Parade she had come upon him. The sea held his eyes until there was no mistaking the footsteps. Her approaching crinoline made soft little rustles, as if entreating him to leave his musings. Her body-guard's shuffles, too, were unmistakable. Like some young potentate her lover turned about, describing an elaborate bow with his white castor. The very picture of starched tranquillity he looked, but underneath the blue hammer-tail coat a heart was beating wildly, as she, made wise by love, knew well—for her own was its echo.

There was a brief moment while she watched the color mount to his sun-bronzed face, the blue eyes glow, the strong form quiver ever so slightly. Then her lips framed "Richard"—the key of the universe. "Patricia!" came the answer.

Juma, from his discreet distance, heard her compared to the magnolia worn on the lapel of the coat she admired so much. In her white and fragrant young womanhood she was like it from sheer inaccessibility. The flower expressed her character and position—Patricia Knickerbocker, a daughter of the autocrat of York. When he mentioned her father's name the girl shivered. An invisible wall seemed to rise between them. Then the feeling died away. Her soul grew wider awake each moment her lover gazed at her.

As he drew her closer to him Juma's figure in the background bent over a flower in the path.

"Let 'em kiss," he mumbled. "Ole Miss used to say de female dat never lub am a sour pippin, and dere's enough ter start a vinegar press in dis family."

"You'll not permit them to take you away from me? You will be mine forever and ever?" said the youth.

A sigh of happiness answered him.

"I know I'm poor, Patricia, and my family can never equal yours."

"Don't!" she whispered. "What does it matter, what does anything matter—only that I'm here *with you*!"

"See the night creeping in off there, dear heart. It holds nothing more wonderful than this moment."

"How black the water looks," she faltered.

"I will go to your father and demand your hand." She was trembling.

"You do not know what a Knickerbocker is—an awful creature with a hundred gorgon heads constantly leering and preaching; detecting flaws in other people's families. One head will tell you that you play the organ in St. Paul's, and another may see that your coat is a trifle worn. We're not the only clan of them in the land."

"We must not fear them—not to-night, when love is filling the world."

"Only one of my grandmothers married for love, and she was thought to be disgraced."

"You will follow her?" he asked, a catch in his voice.

Juma was signalling for them to part, and on his forehead she kissed "I will!"

Now alone on the dark staircase she meditated on his words. When that malignant crone, Gossip, started on her round, what would happen?

Suddenly the voice of her father adding up the indigo cargo fell upon her ears. He would end their happiness; a man powerful enough to kill the spirit of Easter in his home could do anything. Creeping through the narrow passage she came to the great north balcony window. There she paused and raised her eyes to the dome of the night. Long lines of stars were strung across the meadows of heaven. The dials of the world seemed suddenly stilled. Below the infinite peace a budding landscape sloped gently into a placid sea. Myriads of little lights in humble cots blinked an answer to the fires above. Leaning on the broad window-seat of blackened Jersey oak she tried to descry his dwelling, but the tree-tops shut it away.

A few hours before, he had asked her to be his wife, and she, a Knickerbocker, had thrilled at his words. Like a tide the memory of his love swept back to her. Then on its surges came the stupor of desolation. The gates of Knickerbocker pride were strong. A second David might fail to force them. All her dreams were fantasies, with no bearing upon reality. All her hopes were sunbeams vanquished by one dark shadow. To her distorted imagination her family seemed accursed. Every face bore some mark of it, even the row of dim portraits in the room below. But, ah! there was one, a face turned to the rafters of the attic, whose bright eyes and red lips knew love untinctured by the dross of the world. In the darkness it rose before her strangely insistent. As in a time-blurred mirror she looked and saw herself, and the feeling, though uncanny, gave her a sense of comfort.

A wind began to sigh in the garden. Through the boxwood maze and barren urns it swept Smiling Flora, sleeping Endymion, and all the fabulous court that had stood there years before the coming of the Knickerbockers grew more humanly colored as the moon passed behind a cloud. Since York had become a queenly city and the wonder of the western world, mute and peacefully passive they had watched the seasons come and go. Countless lovers must have known them. She saw back into the springs, the flower times. Sedan chairs and swaying post-chaises had borne these dainty lovers all away. Oh, strange, sweet thought! She, too, would have to go—with him.

Down by the pale and shivering elms the iron bar of the gate clicked. Dark figures were entering the garden. The gods and goddesses faded before her eyes. No one visited them on Easter eve. Her father did not keep the season.

She steadied her knees on the slippery seat. The spray of arbutus she was wearing over her heart cut her hands as she pressed closer to the pane.

"My aunts! they know!" she whispered to herself.

Terror of her father—of them all—swept over her, chilling the very recesses of her being. As the habiliments of her august relatives became more distinct, she grew calmer. With slow and measured tread they walked, while to their right minced Betty, a small abigail, swaying a lantern.

"It is the march of pride coming to crush me!" she cried.

Then the bells began to peal again—"Pride—pride" they seemed to mock. "Love must die for pride!"

CHAPTER TWO

On the wreck of many social thrones—for the town named after the Duke of York passed through numerous transitions the world knows nothing of—Patricia's aunt, Miss Georgina Knickerbocker, had elected to raise her sceptre. "I rule by right" was her dictum. "My family is old; few families are older or more aristocratic. The famous Judge Josiah Knickerbocker was my father, and my brother Jonathan owns Knickerbocker Mansion, the finest dwelling in York."

No potentate ever wore a crown more blissfully than Miss Georgina. Tall, beak-nosed, gruff-voiced she was, always with her younger sister, Miss Julie, in tow and under good control—Miss Julie, who smirked and copied her when family pride was concerned, though she had her own misgivings and opinions on other matters. Miss Julie even had emotions and sentimentalities of her own, which she struggled to keep bottled up before her relatives and the world, uncovering them only in secret, as she did her jasmine scent and pomatum pot.

The little woman's real name was Jerusalem, bestowed upon her at a time when the judge her father's religious spirit was in its blossoming period. One great grief of her life was that she had given way to wickedness and changed this outlandish cognomen. She often brought the subject up before Dr. Slumnus, as he stopped in for a social game of chess. "Indeed, Miss Julie," he would answer soothingly, "the name is so Christian that it sounds heathenish. No well-conducted female should presume to bear the name of the holy city. Nay, ma'am, it would have come perilously near sacrilege to retain it!"

Thus assured, Miss Julie would give herself over to the excitement of endeavoring to queen a pawn. Later, in her chamber, ready to blow out her candle, alone with the crowd of memories waiting to conduct her to the land of dreams, she shuddered. Her father's stern eyes would glare at her reproachfully; sometimes she would try to mock at them, remembering the words of Dr. Slumnus—but oftener a tear or two trickled down her faded cheeks and stained the strings of her nightcap.

Together these two elderly Knickerbockers were unweary in their efforts to interpret high life to their circle. Their family pride was more expansive than their brother Jonathan's. He talked chiefly of his Aunt Jane, the milk-weed lady, of his renowned father, and of that dim shade of a Knickerbocker who was the friend of Lord Cornbury. Miss Georgina had climbed higher into her hereditary tree. She prated of a great-uncle who married a niece of Lord Campbell—a cousin underscored in her records as Laird of Barula—the grand Makemies, the high-stepping Gabies, and the learned Gobies. And, as for Aunt Jane, why, she was dowered with a larger chest of silver than any Jersey woman of her day. Those records of her paduasoys and alamodes would have sickened a Custis; and her love-affairs!—the wench herself might have been astounded at hearing that she once refused a patroon of Rensselaerswyck and a president of the College of New Jersey.

Quietly Miss Julie would sit and listen to her sister, but, once away from her, she would assume what she believed to be the Almack manner, call imagination to her aid, and discourse to her long-suffering acquaintance. Aunt Jane's chest of plate became a veritable crown furgeon laden with tasters, posset cups, punch-bowls, muffineers, and salvers of priceless and unique patterns. Her gowns would have done credit to a Drury Lane queen. The patroon of Rensselaerswyck drank a flask of camphor to forget his Jane. Scores of suitors died of lacerated hearts for her dear sake, and the president of the College of New Jersey vowed he could not hear the word love spoken in his presence, not even in his young gentlemen's conjugations.

It was the arrival, from the vulgarian camp of Trenton, of one Mrs. Snograss that first brought interference with the sway of these gentle ladies. That year, in which Richard Sheridan first played the organ in St. Paul's and Mrs. Snograss elected to reside in York, proved, indeed, an eventful one for the community. The genteel portion of Gotham society, like the family of the Vicar of Wakefield, was wont to lead a peaceful life. Most of its adventures befell it by its own fireside, or consisted of migrations from the blue bed to the brown. Or there was the yearly glimpse of the Branch, or Schooley's Mountain, and on rare occasions venturesome parents took their offspring to Hobuck for a fortnight—especially if they were marriageable daughters.

The Misses Knickerbocker had visited the latter place in its transition period. There Georgina purchased her Davenport tea-service for a song, and was fond of telling of the fact. And Julie treasured a sweeter memory of the green Elysium—a dried-up flower of memory, but once a rose, nevertheless, carefully guarded from the world, hidden indeed from herself most of the time.

No one knew exactly how it began—that social war over the two capitals of Trenton and York. Black "Rushingbeau," the York pronunciation for Mrs. Snograss's serving-man, Rochambeau, meeting Juma at the morning market in the centre of the green, had dubbed the Knickerbocker chickens "spinkle-shanked fowls."

"Wot you know 'bout hens in yo' small 'count town!" retorted the loyal champion of York. Like a mushroom the story grew, and spread from Vesey Street kitchens into sitting-rooms and parlors. Of course the aspersive attitude toward York was that of Mrs. Snograss reflected in Rochambeau.

"To think that a resident of Trenton, a city named after a mere merchant, should have the effrontery to speak disparagingly of our ancient capital!" cried Mrs. Rumbell, mother-in-law of Dr. Slumnus. "These are degenerate times, alack! What would poor Roberta Johnstone say if she were here? Let me see how many royal governors have lived amongst us."

Mrs. Rumbell counted on her slim, old fingers. The Knickerbocker ladies, who lacked the Rumbell knowledge of their city's past, brought all their brightest family banners to the fray.

"Lud," said Miss Georgina, and Miss Julie promptly echoed her, "I have never even visited the spot where the Snograss woman came from; I know that the Comte de Survilliers, or plain Mr. Bonaparte, as he prefers to be called, when he failed to secure Knickerbocker Mansion for a residence decided to repair thither. Poor man, he must have languished!" she added with a final snort.

"And he was such a showy man too!" sighed her sister.

Mrs. Snograss, learning of the ferment her servant had aroused, sagaciously remarked: "Let them talk; their chatter is a lecture to the wise; as for capitals, everybody knows, counting out the inhabitants of this mud-hole, that Trenton came near being the capital of the whole country!"

When this bombastic statement was hurled at Vesey Street, it made as much of a sensation as the late news from Cherubusco. Most of the Government officers were classed with the Snograss widow by the affronted Gothamites, and Mrs. Rumbell said openly that if she had her life to live over England should have welcomed her when the cross of St. George was torn down from the courthouse flag-staff.

The winter died and still there was no cessation of hostilities. The choir-room of St. Paul's, where the ladies of the Bengal mission met and listened to itinerant lecturers, or sewed garments for the needy, was the usual field for battle. When Mrs. Snograss arrived late one day for Mr. Timbuckey's talk on the piety of George Crabbe, she was unfortunately ushered to Miss Georgina Knickerbocker's bench. That haughty lady, the enemy being comfortably ensconced, arose and stalked over to Mrs. Rumbell's seat, followed by her sister and the Mansion girls, so that the bustle ensuing spoke to everybody of what was taking place. Patricia smiled a mortified, half sad smile at Mrs. Snograss, but the Trentonian only accepted it as additional insult.

A month later Mrs. Rumbell fainted when her sewing-chair was placed by the disturber of her peace. She was one of the most violent in her aversion to the newcomer. The Rev. Samuel Slumnus shook his fat finger at his mother-in-law, as the crafty dowager, enjoying the excitement created by her feigned swoon, could see with her eyes half-opened. Such conduct was not to be borne. "Rebellion in my own family," fumed the perplexed dominie. "I must put a stop to it at once." In his agitation he clasped and unclasped his hands and caressed his sparse locks. When a hush fell at last upon the room, he was seen mounting the choir-platform.

"The meeting of the Easter Guild will be held this year at the residence of Mrs. Snograss," he sputtered. For a full minute silence reigned—then came a clangor of tongues. "He is almost as red in the face as if he choked on the prune-pits in the Knickerbocker fruit-cake," some irreverent one whispered. It was said afterward that Mrs. Snograss had put a five-dollar bill in the mission-box as she left the choir-room that morning—a performance not without effect. A few parishioners were even heard to lament the fact that Dr. Slumnus's family was not of the same standing as his wife's. Miss Georgina declared privately to her sister that any one who went to the Snograss woman's should never darken the door of Goby House again. But when the day preceding Easter came, and she heard from Julie of the delight the town was taking in the prospect of viewing the much-talked of Snograss interior, one venturesome housekeeper having even asserted that she intended going up to the chambers, Miss Georgina, wild with jealousy, decided to carry the war into the enemy's country.

As the night before that day of days died away and clarion cocks made the young dawn vocal, eager hands drew back the curtains of four-posters. Above the green-gray of spring-time streets and lanes, the sentinel tree-tops pointed to the translucent blue of a smiling sky. "Day's fair and all's well!" bawled the watch as they blew out their smoking lights. Voices cracked and rusted by sleep echoed the cry in the depths of soft, chintz-bound coverlets. "My best ferrandine coat," mumbled Miss Georgina to herself, in her delight over a pleasing picture of her entrance into the Snograss parlor. She let the bolster slip to the floor and precipitated her head against the carved laurel leaves of the top-board, all unconsciously. Bright were the visions of cherished falafals and gewgaws that came to the members of the Easter Guild as they parted company with Morpheus.

Mrs. Rumbell, looking from a casement in the rectory, felt the sweetness of the season fall upon her. That patch of fresh sky, suggestive of new life and a swift-footed May, was more to her than a volley of sermons. The snow still lay on hill and heath. Father Winter, neglectful of one of his worlds, was sporting among the northern mountains. Oh, the peace of it! Why should she care if the wealthy Mrs. Snograss had come to York with her Trenton innovations? All her past grievances were forgotten. In her blissful state she felt she could even go the length of sewing whalebone in her second-best silk skirt to conform to the ridiculous fashion of stiffened skirts, introduced by that lady. Everything was changing! What could she, frail and old, gain by wrestling with the times? Across the way, torn landscape shades blinded the windows of Johnstone House. Roberta was dead and her home awaited a new tenant. Beyond lay the Bowling Green, the background of her long life—witness to all the parts the stage-master, Fate, had dealt out to her. Joys and sorrows marked its worn paths. The city of her golden time was fading away. No halloos of eager huntsmen, ushering in Aurora, greeted her ears as of yore. Only a stray thrush, mistaking the season, trilled liquid notes to his lost mates on a hemlock by her chamber.

Soon the daylight's eyes were wide open, and the door-knockers, across the church-yard, began to glow like miniature suns. Festivals and holidays always brought the housekeepers of York to market, followed by their faithful blacks carrying little wicker baskets. They tripped first to Mrs. Sykes's booth, where one could find all the season's delicacies; then to the wintergreen-berry man, and on through the circle of venders. The mystical joy of Eastertide that flooded the heart of Mrs. Rumbell in the dawn swept through the concourse at the market. The perfume of the southern lilies, the merry cries of hucksters, and the shrill calls of gutter-waifs as they tugged at the skirts of Cock-a-nee-nae Bess were all permeated with it.

The prattling groups about Mrs. Sykes ofttimes broke away to take sly looks across the green at the distant Broadway. "Will she come?" "Shall we extend our hands to her, or just curtesy?" These and many like questions went for naught that morning. The blinds of Snograss house were parted; a turbaned negress came out and washed the entry. Once the opening of a door thrilled the curious dames. But the newcomer was waiting to enjoy her full triumph in the afternoon.

No one looked toward the house on Vesey Street. The Knickerbockers never frequented the market—Jonathan Knickerbocker forbade his family's participation in such vulgar customs.

Georgina did not descend to her sitting-room in as pleasant a humor as was to have been expected from her waking contemplations. She jangled her keys so ominously as she strutted through the halls and pantries that Julie was afraid to venture out. On the day before Easter the little woman was in the habit of stealing away to a by-lane near the market. From a discreet distance she directed her purchases. Children would run for her oranges, the cock-a-nee-nae necessary to her happiness, the boxes of Poppleton sweets and foreign nuts. When they were very swift she would reward them with as much as a dime apiece, so great was the delight she felt in providing a secret store of goodies.

To-day there was no escaping. The market was sold out and the booths carried away before she finished helping her sister tie up the Easter presents. It was a custom among the ladies of York to exchange chaste and useful gifts of their own handiwork. Worsted hat-bag covers and silk mittens were the favorites. Mrs. Rumbell was the one exception to the rule. She still cut up her father's brocade vests into small squares, which she filled with dried rose-geranium leaves and distributed among her acquaintance. Three generations had received these fragrant marks of her regard, and the wits accused her relative of having been a Hollander, addicted to the habit of swarthing himself in superfluous garments. Members of the Scruggins set went further, and hinted maliciously that he was a dealer in old clothes.

Miss Georgina preferred silk mittens, and gave and received no less than a dozen pairs a season. If the ones sent to her were of a color she did not like, she kept them for a year or two, and then packed them off again. This was quite permissible in York. On one occasion Georgina's own mittens were returned to her, but far from being angry, she smiled a grim welcome at them, and remarked to her household that she was glad to see them back for they were at least fashioned of pure silk, and that was more than she could say of many pairs that had been sent to her.

Quaint little ladies of Gothamtown—quaint little old-time figures!—flitting in and out of your ancient homes like shadows!—who cares to-day for your petty gifts, your plans, and jealousies? Only one or two remember you. The walks you trod are vanishing, the water-front gardens where you smiled and languished at sedate gentlemen are mostly hidden 'neath bricks and mortar, and the very buildings you were born in, that stood so long impervious to the rude hands of progress, are being demolished. Those musty garments of Juma's "ole Miss," the friend of Mrs. Rumbell, are now folded in some attic trunk with your own pet vanities. What would the haughty Miss Georgina have said if she could have gazed through the door of the future and seen a Scruggins brat grown into a leader of fashion and carrying her own tortoise fan—sold with other Knickerbocker effects at the last vendue?

If one had loitered in Vesey Street that afternoon before Easter so many years past, one would, no doubt, have joined the stragglers about the gates of Snograss House, and watched the members of St. Paul's Easter Guild mince up Broadway, carefully keeping to the pave. The Flying Swan from Elizabethtown was due at four o'clock, and those timid ladies of the long ago knew that the swaying, swaggering bedlam of a coach would enjoy spattering them as it rattled up to the City Hotel. On the porch of that fine hostelry, where Mr. Clarke once wooed his muse and scores of thirsty throats the wine-cup, stood the host, Davy Juniper, whose very name was synonymous with cheer. Through the half-opened door came loud gusts of unceremonious laughter as the portly innkeeper, curveting on tiptoe, swung his garland of Easter green over the sign-board. Davy's eyes were riveted on the flashing colors of feminine gear across the street. Now Mrs. Rumbell tottered by and bobbed to him; now a bevy of the Scruggins set passed the house opposite, and gazed in, like forbidden Peris at the door of Paradise. Sometimes the street was covered with pedestrians. The quality abroad affected the good man's spirits. He began to pipe some merry verses from a tap-room ditty:

Major Macpherson heav'd a sigh, Tol, de diddle, dol, dol; And Major Macpherson didn't know why, Tol, de diddle, dol, dol; But Major Macpherson soon found out, Tol, de diddle, dol, dol; 'Twas all for Miss Lavinia Scout, Tol, de diddle, dol, dol.

The night was creeping on, clear and cold, and there would be full settles about his waggish fires. In the sky, puffs of fleecy clouds were hurrying away like sheep eager to reach the fold of mother-dusk. Off in the west, where twilight parted her curtains, glowed faint streaks of yellow and rose color, promises of daffodil meadows and flower-strewn lands to come.

He was turning for a parting survey of the street when his ears caught the tremulous motion of some vehicle. Dashing out of Vesey Street came the Knickerbocker chariot, creaking protestations as it swung up to the Snograss stile.

Out popped Miss Georgina, followed by her sister. Never had Miss Georgina seemed so like a man-of-war's man in a flounce. Miss Julie shrunk into insignificance beside her. Tavern maids, attracted by the noise and heedless of the cold, poked their heads out of dormer windows. The passengers on the Flying Swan just turning the pike slipped cautiously from the seats behind the guard to find out the cause of the excitement. Juma, hurrying home to the mansion, paused for a moment to see the sisters of his master step down. "Ramrods—old Ramrods," jeered Mr. Juniper, as he flung a last defiant "tol, de rol," at the gaping street.

The door of the tavern had no more than swung to when that of Snograss House opened. Every inmate of the room eyed Miss Georgina as she greeted the mistress. There was an element of hostility in their ceremonious handshake. As the sister of the autocrat of York viewed the rich furnishings of the apartment, the gold-legged piano and the silk-covered furniture, her lips straightened into a sinister line. Her own possessions shrunk into insignificance compared with this elegance. Even the long shut-up state parlor in Knickerbocker Mansion could hardly vie with it. Lady Tyron, the last lady of York, had fitted that room with heirlooms from her English home. Jonathan was in the habit of calling it the finest apartment in the State. He prated of its mouldering beauties often, forgetting that it was lauded by his townsmen long before the Knickerbockers entered its portals.

The contents of the Snograss parlor had given other Gothamites momentary uneasiness that afternoon. Of course no one felt they possessed the Knickerbocker right to feel deeply aggrieved over them. Mrs. Rumbell, spying the oil-painted views of Trenton by the entrance door, hurriedly shut her eyes, vowing the calm feeling in her heart should not be disturbed. As penance for the pain which the pictures of the hated capital gave her she seized a dish of quince scones and ran with them to Dr. Slumnus. Refreshments had not been passed about, and the rector of St. Paul's signalled to his mother-in-law not to approach. Thinking that he preferred the gooseberry tarts on an opposite table she hastened over for them, until

Samuel, visibly embarrassed by her attentions, left his comfortable cushioned chair and took refuge in the hall.

If any one had imagined that Mrs. Snograss would forgive the various slights put upon her in York, she or he was doomed to disappointment. All the pleasant things they said to her about her costly egg-shell china, the glass aviary with the artificial tree, and other luxuries, failed to soften her vindictive mood. Each timidly expressed compliment recalled to her a covert sneer, a deprecating smile, or a garment hastily drawn aside. As Miss Georgina, on behalf of the presiding committee, counted up the Easter gifts the church would give to the poor, the Trenton widow whom she feared as a rival was musing on past insults.

"Ten tin trumpets," called the loud voice.

"I can humble her," thought the Snograss woman.

"Ten surprise packages," continued the other.

"I'll give the Knickerbocker family a surprise," spoke the indignant Trentonian half aloud.

She was naturally an amiable person, but the aristocratic congregation of St. Paul's had impaired her temper, proffering her vinegar when she had sought the wine of good-fellowship. She stared at the bedizened figure of the sister of the autocrat of York a moment longer, then turned meaningly to the only member of the Scruggins set who happened to be present. There was already a look of triumph in her eyes. "She shall bend to the dust soon," she whispered. Then she arose from her sofa, clashing the folds of her tilter until the room was full of lustring mockery. Everything was in readiness for Mrs. Snograss's climax of the afternoon. Revenge spread out its hands and gave her tongue.

"Have you ever heard of 'The School for Scandal,' Miss Knickerbocker?" she asked, wreathing her face in an inscrutable smile.

Glad of an opportunity for displaying her knowledge, Georgina rose eagerly to the bait. "I saw the play at the Park in the twenties. 'Twas a prodigious fine cast, if I remember."

"They say a new Sheridan has come to our city." Every Gothamite loved that phrase, "our city," and Mrs. Snograss dwelt on the words with the nicest shade of mimicry. "He is preparing a little comedy I might dub the same name," she snickered.

"An author man?" asked the Knickerbocker voice that always filled the room. "What does he want here?"

A sudden silence fell upon the company. Eyes were turned on the Turkey carpet before the fireplace where the great ladies stood. Ears were cocked in their direction. The pirouetting woodland fay embellishing the tambour firescreen, worked by the Trentonian when she attended Madame de Foe's Academy for gentle children, wore a more conscious smirk than usual. Even the twin Bow dogs which had held their tufted tails erect through the stormiest family fracases seemed agitated.

"He plays the organ at our church," she answered with forced deliberation; then in a whisper loud enough to have done credit to a lady on the boards, she added, "and when away from that instrument spends his time making love to your niece Patricia."

Mrs. Snograss gave a hysterical laugh and retreated a few rods.

A thunder-bolt falling at Miss Georgina's feet could not have created more consternation. For a moment she glared at the creature before her as if she were a butterfly or a beetle—something to be crushed and killed —then remembering that politeness is always a trusty weapon, she roared in as soft a fashion as she could, "You are mistaken, madam!"

"My Julie saw them kissing less than an hour ago on the Marine Parade!"

"Ladies who make confidants of their servants are often misinformed," the other hissed.

By this time all Vesey Street was on its feet. The plans of the day were forgotten. Every one was too stunned to speak. A Knickerbocker openly insulted—the thought was appalling! Miss Julie, who was fingering some Snograss ambrotypes, let them slip to the floor in her excitement. She had not been so much agitated for years—not since a certain ship sailed out of Amboy for the Indies bearing a youthful captain whom Judge Knickerbocker had bidden her forget.

"Oh, oh!" she gasped—and there were those who afterward declared she looked almost pleased. "My niece has a lover!" But in another breath, "Oh, what will her father say?"

"Jerusalem, restrain yourself," called her sister. That lady was sweeping proudly from the room.

"My Julie saw them kissing less than an hour ago on the marine parade"

"Impudence!" she said, thrusting her sister out of the hall. When the cold air of the street touched their hot faces, she spoke again. Her anger was fast engulfed in a wave of bitter humiliation.

"We are disgraced, Jerusalem! The Knickerbocker name dishonored! The man is a person of common family. I fear the Gobies and the Gabies are turning in their graves. What would Aunt Jane have thought?"

"They kissed in the shrubbery—My niece in love?" Miss Julie was whispering to herself unheeded. The faded leaves of the one flower in her heart were stirring gently.

Now and then the faint note of a bell drifted on the air. The old sexton of St. Paul's was preparing his metal children for their long anthem.

"Oh, joyous night, make haste—make haste," they tinkled to the taper-like star above them.

"Disgraced!" muttered Miss Georgina.

CHAPTER THREE

The glimmering lantern which the serving-maid Betty carried seemed like a huge firefly come back to a land of blooms. Sometimes in dim alleyways it caught in her flapping garments, and her two mistresses were forced to cling together until they reached the next patch of moonlight. When their half-tasted dinner was finished, and the silver counted and locked in the cherry cabinet, Georgina commanded her sister to step over with her to the mansion. Jonathan never permitted the family vehicle to be brought out when the world was not looking, and his womenkind were used to tramping through the darkness. Julie was reluctant to go at first, but the other's anger flamed so high she could not help catching some of the sparks.

"Would you allow your niece to ruin her life by marrying a man who gains his livelihood playing a musical instrument? Methinks you have a fondness for hornpipers and such. There was Signor Succhi, our dancing-master, I recollect"—nodding her head—"he used to call you 'little peach-blossom'—his little peach-blossom!"

Julie smiled at Georgina's latest feat of memory; then she turned about and gazed into the dying embers. For a moment she stood beside a merry-eyed youth who dared her to prick the signor's silken calves. Did he really perfect their symmetry with cotton as was said, she wondered? Alas, that she was born timorous.

"Are your wits leaving you, Jerusalem?" continued the other—"you who wear Aunt Jane's hair locket and have been for years an ornament in the highest sphere of this city—now being ruined by Trentonians and other foreigners. Where is your boasted allegiance to those of your family who have gone before you?"

Threatened and cajoled by turns Miss Julie was led into the night. "The Snograss woman may have lied," came the consoling thought. She cheered herself with it hurrying through the snow.

Up Church Street they stumbled past huts and houses. Warm windows beckoned to them. Georgina had forgotten the mittens for her nieces. The scene at the Snograss House was uppermost in her mind. "What a sly minx Patricia is to have kept the disgraceful affair from us so long," she was thinking. "Could that skulking Juma have helped her? He knew enough to bamboozle one. There was a report that old Roberta Johnstone even read him novels." The boisterous wind, tossing the budding lilac branches about the statues in the Knickerbocker garden which the girl in the window-seat was watching, came shrieking out of unexpected openings and buffeted her aunts in the face.

Now they were entering the narrow passage that opened into Vesey Street. The tavern lights twinkled beyond, but drear and lonely the artery for cut-throats appeared.

Georgina, brave and intrepid, was still nursing her wrath when a mist came before her eyes. "I see! I feel queer!" she cried. Her companions were shaking like autumn leaves. "Oh, don't pause, sister!" squeaked terrified Julie, "here's where that picaroon in the black mask was wont to hide. A Dick Turpin may be concealed yonder!"

"Hist!" called Georgina, as if speaking to some vermin of the night. A shadowy mocking face was rising up before her. She began to tremble—where had she seen it? Yes, 'twas the face of the ancestress whose portrait Jonathan took down from the line of Knickerbockers in the parlor. "My nerves," she gasped. "Come, let us haste, you trembling fools!" Once in the driveway to the house she denied her fright. Betty was scolded for stumbling over a brier-bush. When the long flight of steps was reached, she rushed at them boldly. "Knock, Jerusalem," she commanded.

The little woman tried to sound the clapper, then fell back exhausted. Georgina, enraged, seized it and thumped violently upon the plate. The sounds reverberated through the night, clashing against the bell-notes and the sound of the swaying elms.

Jonathan and his daughters sprang from their seats. The Santa Cruz invoices slipped to the floor and fluttered after the wool balls like merchants aspiring to new possessions. What cared the horn of plenty on the door for the profits of the Fleet Sally? It had watched the ebb and flow of lordlier fortunes. "That ear-splitting bell hubbub—and now visitors," said the master, advancing to his offspring as if they were the cause of this new annoyance.

Juma, already half-drunk with dreams, rubbed his dazed head and hastened toward the entry. Was Toussaint calling him? Did the chair of Marie du Buc de Marcinelle, the Elizabethtown beauty, pause before the hair-dresser's sign? Then time and place came back. Realizing that he was watched, he drew the great bolt with a show of strength, and in bounded the gale-blown humanity.

"You?" queried the head of the Knickerbockers. That was the only greeting he gave his nearest relations on Easter eve. He glanced at Julie to see whether she secreted any packages about her person.

Georgina, entering the room, her face stern and white, said, eyeing him, "Prepare yourself for a shock."

He returned the challenge.

Had she been tampering with her five-per-cents for Peruvian investments? Was it the old plaint—Jerusalem's frivolity? Why did the woman gaze at him so mournfully?

"Prepare yourself," she continued, her voice rising to a shriek. "Patricia—your Patricia—has disgraced us!"

The girl peering from the landing heard her name called. Her secret was known to the world and would soon be an implement of torture. The arbutus fell from her bodice unheeded. She could not meet that cruel group below!

"Richard," sighed the stray gusts of wind on the staircase; "Richard" chimed the patient clock. She crept closer to the baluster railing. Some mysterious force was guiding—impelling her onward. Out of the shadows flashed a face. Like a smile it vanished. She ran to the steps. For a moment she stood silent, gaining courage to descend.

At the very moment when she had glanced back tremblingly for a parting benediction from the stars, a figure wrapped in a great-coat was hurrying out of the Sheridan garden. It was Patricia's lover. The youth often came to gaze at her home after sleep locked all the doors of the world but the dream door for which he had never yet found a key. Then the daytime's barriers were broken and she was his alone. Under the Knickerbocker elm-trees he would stand, sometimes, a wild, impassioned troubadour, aflame with songs of love for his imprisoned mate. Again she came to him a vision pure and ethereal and he folded her to his heart in memory of one perfect Junetime day—while multitudes of roses shed their fragrant petals and birds trilled a divine chorus. To-night, with the wondrous Easter peace upon him, she seemed to walk by his side. Those bell-notes drifting on the air were the music of their lives. Hand in hand they floated on the flow of the darkness. Through the days—and the years. Through the springs—and the summers. Always together! Little forms clutched their knees. Carking care crept out of black coverts. Death beckoned to them in the distance—still, there was the scent of Junetime roses. Ah, God! those roses of love, they were theirs for all eternity!

As he neared Knickerbocker Mansion his mood changed. The bells were dying away again. Old Jenkins up in the steeple above the lights of the drowsy city was letting his metal children rest. Their task would soon be over, for the faithful moss-hung clock already pointed to the nightcap hour. The rushes in the poorer regions near the waste lands were flickering out—only the gentry street was still aglow.

A flock of snow-sparrows caught by the gale dashed past the youth, chattering bird imprecations. Beyond, in the moonlight, loomed Her dwelling-place. Coldly white and dreary it looked. Everything about it was mute and unaware of the joyous night. Did Juma keep his promise and give her the arbutus? A longing thrilled him to know her thoughts at this hour. Were they of him? He hastened into the carriage-path, following the footprints made by the trio from Goby House. The leaden statues leered at him in the spaces between the evergreens. Bare shrubs sighed their gusty dirges at his heels.

At the lordly flight of steps he paused and hesitated. Then her pleading voice seemed to rise on the wind. A strange intuition swayed him. The great door of the mansion was moving, opening inward. He asked himself if he were going stark mad, as he crept to it softly, like a thief.

A cry met his ears, and he staggered back—"I love him! I shall love him always!" came the words.

"Patricia," he whispered breathlessly.

Before him was the dismal length of the hall that he had never hoped to enter. Slowly he reeled forward.

While her lover was coming to her through the night, the girl was descending the staircase. At the bottom she paused and remained very still. From the room beyond an army of candle rays was slipping underneath the green sarcenet curtain and capering gnome-like about her feet. They were waiting for her in there! A prowling rat scampered down the dark passage. In another moment she would stand before her indignant family. The curtain shifted and shadows chased away the light. Behind the awful thing were their watchful eyes. She began to tremble and stretch out her hands imploringly at the space before it. The courage that had brought her so near to the chamber of judgment was fast vanishing when Juma came slowly out of the pantry. He did not speak, but his sad old eyes rested on her lovingly. Stifled sobs shook her slender frame as she nestled close to him, seeking the help that he was powerless to give. A wilder gust of wind blew the neglected spray of arbutus from the landing above and it fell at her feet like a message. She looked at it a moment, then slowly parted the veil of the inevitable. The eyes she feared were now upon her.

Jonathan, choleric with indignation, stood by his desk, clenching his hands. At the sight of the child whose conduct swept aside every Knickerbocker law his rage overflowed, and the room was full of a torrent of reproaches. Once he came near knocking over a bust of Mr. Washington, the property of a Makemie, and Miss Julie gave a slight scream.

Patricia heard him silently. She was calmer than any of the spectators. The other Mansion girls continually slid off their chairs and made weird gurgles with their throats. Several times they almost interrupted their parent. As for Georgina, her high-built hair shook like a barrister's wig in the heat of a court appeal.

"You have disgraced us—a common follower fit for a tire-woman! Yes, miss, in your veins flows the Knickerbocker blood, though I cannot credit it. Say 'tis a lie ere I turn you out. Say 'tis the fabrication of that catamount Trenton woman, envious of your aunts' reputation. Speak, girl! Is it true that the town has seen you keeping trysts with him at the Battery? Speak!" gasped the worthy man.

"It is true," said Patricia, trying to keep herself strong for battle.

The draught from the half opened door, which Juma in his excitement had neglected to shut, swept the chimney piece and ended the life of a candle.

"Look!" said Jonathan dragging his daughter by the arms, and pointing to the portraits along the wall. "You are the first to disgrace them! They were as fine a line of men and women as was ever bred up in America. Think you they stepped down from their high places for silly fancies? Think you they forgot they were born to superior circumstances and sullied their reputations?"

Here the autocrat of York's voice broke slightly. The same ghostly face that had appeared to Miss Georgina in Cut-throat Alley leered at him suddenly, and he recoiled. Aghast, he remembered the painting under the attic eaves!

Patricia was facing him. The word love was in his ears. With a maddened cry he advanced quivering. Along the films of the air he saw his ancestors as he often pictured them to himself—a fine mass of superior clay on a pedestal.

"You shall give him up!" he thundered. Then he turned. The green sarcenet curtain moved ominously, and the form of Richard Sheridan was disclosed in its folds.

The youth, heedless of the frowning faces about him, gazed only at the woman he was ready to die for if need were. The passions of the world were swept away as the echo of her cry "I love him—I shall love him always!"—bounded through his heart. For one harmonious moment they gazed into each other's eyes forgetful of surging discords. With stronger grip he clutched at the curtain!

"You, sirrah!" scoffed the voice Patricia thought would go on forever, inflicting fresh wounds at each new outburst. "Impudent organ thumper—to dare come here! I'll better your judgment." As he moved nearer Richard she thrust herself before him.

From the corner of the room came a wail from Julie. "Oh, don't be hard on them, Jonathan. You helped father make me give up Captain MacLeerie," she faltered. "I might have been Mrs. Captain MacLeerie! Poor Bodsey—he vowed he'd never sail a ship into Amboy Harbor again—and perhaps the cannibals have him now, or the devil fishes!"

She began to weep softly. Outside a heavy oaken shutter clanked against the house. Patricia threw her arms about her lover's neck, and her father gazed at her spellbound with fury.

"Disgraced us, hussy," he muttered. "Go with your tinker!"

Juma fell on his knees and began to lament after the fashion of his kind.

"Begone!"—spoke the voice again, breaking at last—"You are no longer one of us!"

The girl, supported by the man to whom she was giving her young life, and followed by the trembling negro, crept slowly away.

Whiffs of air increasing to a current swept from out the hall. The remaining lights fought with it—then despaired. A tired moon was slumbering behind the western pines, and only the glow of a few watchful stars dripped through the casements.

Simultaneously the breaths of every one in the room came faster and faster. Vapors wan and tinged with dust filled the atmosphere, and an unmistakable odor of sandal-wood, faint from long imprisonment.

The startled Knickerbockers retreated to the walls, knocking over chairs and tables in their flight. Before the green sarcenet curtain which had played such a part in the affairs of the night there was a waft of airy garments. A white weft of towering hair—black, burning eyes. Three Knickerbockers knew them! The lady of the banished portrait was moving through the doorway and speaking in quaint last-century utterance.

"Come back!" she called to the lovers, speaking to Patricia. "'Tis a weary while I have been in the other world, but your sore need has brought me here on the anniversary of the birth of love. I am your great-great-grandmother, who felt the full force of the pretty passion and stole away with my dear heart from yonder theatre in old John Street—a grain house in your time, so one from York who recently joined us informed me.

"The lady of the banished portrait was moving through the doorway"

"Although my likeness does not hang in the family line, I bear you small malice. I get a surfeit of their society." Here the ghost sighed, and with the saddest air possible tapped her empty snuffbox and went through the act of inhaling a reviving pinch of strong Spanish. "This girl who has the bloom of me I would befriend, and as the greatness of your ancestors is all that stands in the way of a marriage with the man of her choice, I have bid them come to meet you and get their opinions, mayhap."

A tremor went through the room! More unearthly visitants? The flesh was creeping on the bones of all the living Knickerbockers!

"They are waiting for us in Lady Knickerbocker's state room yonder—Sir William tried to kiss me there once after a junket," she continued. "He would not come to-night—I fear he was afraid it would be dull."

She moved over to Jonathan, who was speechless from fright, and laid a shadowy hand on his. Once past the door ledge she began the descent of the hall as if footing the air of some ancient melody. With grim, rebellious face the present head of her house moved with her, apparently against his own volition.

By the one brightly floriated mirror she straightened her osprey plumes and tapped him gently with her fan. "You dance like a footman," she said. "Have you go-carts 'neath your feet?"

The trembling file of Knickerbockers followed after them, seemingly blown by the wind, whose diabolical wailing reverberated through the house. Doors and windows raged and rattled. There were stridulous, uncanny groans from quaking beams. Behind the panels adown the hall rose and swelled the confused murmur of many voices. The echoes of long dead years were reviving. Above them all was a dying requiem of bells, tolling low and mournfully like a warning to belated road-farers that the ghosts of the haughty Knickerbockers were seeking earth again.

CHAPTER FOUR

s the family neared the long unused state parlor the din grew louder—a rising treble of voices, ascending from hoarse trumpet tones to a twittering falsetto, accompanied by a maddening persistent tapping of high heels on the smooth floor. The sounds of shivering glass as a girandole crashed from its joining met their ears. Each second was a discord running wild with panic-striking incidents.

Julie grasped frantically at the more stalwart Georgina, while clinging to her own garments were the three Mansion girls, screeching like the town's whistles in a March twilight.

The ghost little Jerusalem feared the most was that of the stern Judge. "Will he know that I have changed my name?" she wailed. "Oh, sister, I ate up those bracelets he gave me for taking treacle. I sold them to a silversmith and bought French prunes. You know you said that you'd as soon eat stewed bull-frogs as anything grown by the Monsieurs, and all York was stewing prunes!"

Georgina never turned her head at this remarkable confession. Her features had assumed a strange rigidity; she was as silent as her brother. The shrieks of her nieces, old Juma's incessant lamentations, and the low whispers of the lovers were all unheeded. The racket behind the cobwebbed doors, never opened but for Knickerbocker weddings and funerals, absorbed her senses. Slowly they were swinging back for Jonathan and his phantom partner. The delicate odor of sandal-wood, was strengthened by gasps of musk. Into a yellow blinding glare of light the file of Knickerbockers looked, and their eyes grew gooseberry-like with horror.

A crowd of shades bedecked in their last earthly garniture were gliding and teetering about; some dignified as at a stately farce, others hilarious with ungraceful levity.

As the living Knickerbockers appeared in the room the waggling and chortling fell into a monotone, and the company began to pass in review before them, seemingly desirous of attracting individual notice. Few wore the costly attire one would have expected from the tales spread about them by the Knickerbockers of Vesey Street. Several were clad in plain humhums and torn fustians. One chirpy dame in a moth-eaten tabby hugged a little package of Bohea to her stomacher, unmindful of the fact that the luxury had grown much cheaper since she quitted this sphere. Another, who evidently thought herself a beauty, wore a false frontage of goat hair before her muslin cap, and ogled Jonathan as she passed, though he did not seem eager for a flirtation with his ugly great-aunt.

An ungainly yokel stepped on the feet of the Mansion girls, and some bold gentlemen, who had spent a goodly portion of their natural lives in Bridewell, swore at them. Still the awful procession kept moving on—faces were as thick as the tapers glowing in every bracket and candelabra. Bursts of music rose on the wind—a wheezing tune that sobbed of past jubilation. Suddenly all the Knickerbockers gasped. Stern Judge Knickerbocker, who had rarely smiled in life, was seen advancing, bent double with laughter and clinging to a figure in a cardinal hoop.

"Oh, let us cover our eyes," whispered Miss Georgina. "This is more than I can bear."

"Don't!" said the lady of the banished portrait. "You have often boasted of your family's intimacy with that queer figure. Through your veneration of him, York has made him into quite a hero. It is the friend of one of the first American Knickerbockers—Lord Cornbury! He was addicted to wearing women's furbelows!"

"Gazooks!" exclaimed his Lordship, in a tone loud enough for the Knickerbockers to hear. "More of those tiresome impertinents! The next thing the whole of the presumptuous clan will be petitioning me for standing room at my routs."

"Don't go any nearer to them," said the Judge, in the tones of a sycophant. "If they bore you, my dear Corny, I am willing to cut them. *You know it is the fashion on earth to recognize only the most desirable* ancestors, and we can return the compliment. Besides it was decreed that I should be jocular for the next half century, and I'm afraid a too close inspection would cause me to don weepers."

The group by the doors felt a sickening sensation in their flaccid frames. Jonathan's partner, knowing how grievously they must all have been affected by the change in their parent, turned her head.

A one-eyed hag was advancing to her. She curtsied low, and presented two bits of plaster which had fallen from the ceiling.

"Messages," she snickered, fumbling with her hands.

"From Marmaduke and Leonidas Barula," read the lady (though no one knows how, for she only observed the niches). "We beg to be excused from coming to-night. To put it mildly, we were raised aloft in Pearl Street Hollow for practising target shooting on coach-drivers, and our necks are still out of joint and not fit to be seen in company."

As the merriment waxed louder a Gobie, who had spent her life as a fish-fag, began tapping on the panelled wainscot. With a hoarse guffaw she turned her piercing alaquine eyes on Miss Julie and squinted—"More negus! More here, you slubber-degullions. We Gobies has a thirst. 'Twas what we were noted for in life—not our learning, great-niece," she mocked, as she turned her head and grimaced at Miss Georgina.

"Go away!" snuffled that once resolute woman, too weak to combat any longer. A feeling of despair was settling upon her like a pall. What if Mrs. Rumbell, or, worse still, if Mrs. Snograss should be passing Knickerbocker House and hear the oaths and ungenteel voices of the supposedly elegant family? No tap-room fracas at Fraunces' could have equalled the deafening hubbub.

"Beshrew the old fool, she be as jealous for the lies she told of us as a Barbary pigeon."

"Go away!" continued the sinking sister of the autocrat of York.

That distraught-looking gentleman himself was hastening across the room with restorative salts, which one of his daughters always carried in her reticule. As he approached Georgina the Gobie snatched the bottle from his hand and drained it at a gulp.

"Anything with fire-water for me," she hiccoughed. Then clutching hold of him, she sunk her voice to a whisper—"I left this sphere for drinking a quart of gillyflower scent!"

Julie began to weep softly—"Oh, Aunt Jane, if you were only here! Our Aunt Jane was different from these people," she wailed to herself, half apologetically.

She was fond of studying the picture in the other room and could have traced it from memory. Raising her eyes, she gave a prolonged shriek. The fish-fag and some of the Makemies were dragging her beloved Jane over Lady Lyron's court steps, out of the powdering closet.

The room was becoming uproarious. Doors were opening and shutting again, letting in the moaning of the bells. The culmination of the buffoonery was approaching.

"Good, Jane," sobbed Miss Julie.

"Good, Jane," echoed the chorus of the spectres.

Reluctant, and feigning a great stress of emotion, the poor lady was pushed into the illuminated space below the hundred-taper drop. She looked like some pretty long-vaulted effigy. In her hands she still carried the spray of milk-weed.

The noise lessened for a moment. Jane gazed reproachfully at her niece, Julie, as if the indiscreet wish were the cause of her present misery, and said, in a pensive voice, "I did not want to come to-night."

"I always knew you were a modest woman," said Jonathan, recovering a little of his once audacious manner.

"Modest forsooth!" giggled the fish-fag diabolically, and seizing one of Jonathan's fat hands in her bony fingers, she drew it over the other's face.

"Look, see the white streaks on her now! She reddened, the hussy,—or I'm not a Gobie!"

"Yes, I was vain," answered the most prated-about of female Knickerbockers. "I used countless beautifiers—pearl powders, cherry salve, cupid's tints. Everything Mr. Gaine sold at the Crown. They hooked the men. When pearl powders came upon the market, I received three offers—Jenks—a tutor at King's College—not the President, as the report remains on earth—wrote me a poem in the *Weekly Gossiper*, called 'Pink and White Amanda.'"

"Jane Knickerbocker," said the ghost who was giving the party, "your family has spent many hours telling the present generation of your womanly virtues, and they cannot fail in having an overweening respect for any opinion you may utter. Shall this girl who bears your blood marry yon youth?"

"Let them wed by all means, if they see advantage in it. I vow if I could come back to earth and live my twenty-eight years over again, I would join hands with Jean, our Elizabeth-Town perfumer."

Lord Cornbury and the shades about him were bowed with mirth.

"Janet, you giddy girl, though half the age of most of us, I protest you are becoming a wit. You will be getting into society next," he cried. "I shall never be mean enough to tell that in sublunary times one of the first American Knickerbockers knew me intimately only as my valet."

"A fig for your class distinctions," called the fair indignant, hunting for a rouge rag. "Years ago we heard "twas money made the court circle at York.' Why, you must remember how you feared your creditors when they first came below."

"Alack, indeed," said his Lordship plaintively, "this hooped petticoat was never paid for."

After dishevelled Jane had vanished again into the powdering closet whence she had first emerged, the lady of the banished portrait moved over to Patricia and her lover. Standing side by side the resemblance between the two women was remarkable. One was the budding flower; the other the fragile shadow of a beautiful life.

"Her kind will always exist," she said. "They marry for pearl powders and other vanities, and usually seek, or are forced into, a gilded cage. There, like jackdaws, they call out their possessions from dawn till night, and the heedless world passing by sees the sparkling of the gold, mistakes the caws for singing, and applauds. I knew love—the ideal love that smiles at one from the wayside when one is seeking it in the well-kept gardens. I paid for it with my heart's blood, and I never had cause to regret. Over the rough places of my earthly journey it followed me with radiant illusions. The April winds were sweeter, the sunshine on the roads warmer. I felt all the raptures mother nature gives her children. That is why I could leave the other world to do you this service. *Love* is the one thing death cannot lull to sleep!"

Patricia tried to answer, but the power of speech had left her for the moment. Juma's face was glowing with peaceful smiles. He bent low on his right knee to kiss the diaphanous draperies of the shade.

Outside in the night there arose the low murmurous chanting of the town waits moving homeward. A chime of bells, as soft as a blessing. The thorns had fallen from the brows of love.

While Patricia's benefactress gave her message the circle of ghosts was making way for the other Knickerbockers to enter. On closer inspection, many of them proved to be tame sort of animals enough. From a distance one monster of a woman had given the impression that she was trying to bully posterity. Perhaps this was due to the long feathers in her head-dress, that nodded maliciously at her most placid motion. As she bowed to her descendants a plume tickled the tip of Jonathan's nose and he jumped back slightly. "I am Melodia Mudford Makennie," she said, "and I thought you would like to meet me, as I started the Christmas fashion of giving hot-bag covers in York."

"Hot-bag covers!" reiterated Miss Georgina, astonished. "I have always said mittens. Why, in my ancestry book it is noted that in the year 1768 you gave one hundred pairs of silk mittens to Gruel Hall, the home for tiresome gentlewomen."

"The years play great hoaxes," chuckled the ghost. "Those ancestry books are a standard joke with us, and I believe they are looked upon with some suspicion in your own world."

Melodia seemed so friendly, Julie gained courage enough to purse up her lips for a speech, but the shade anticipated her.

"I know what you are going to ask—why did I make such a wide frill about the bottle's neck? 'Tis easy to explain. I never took my bag to church to warm my hands—'twas my stomach!"

"Oh!" said Miss Julie, faltering slightly, fearing that this relative might become vulgar like the terrible Gobies still dancing about Lord Cornbury.

"Yes," continued the other, "when William fell asleep during the sermon I used to sink down well in the pew, put the frill up to my mouth, squeeze the end of the bag, and get as much as a dram of whiskey."

"Oh!" exclaimed Julie, aghast; "a hot-water bag for whiskey!"

"Why not?" said the ghost, angrily. Her manner was that of one who had expected commendation for her cleverness. The plumes in her head-dress were shaking violently.

"Why not, miss?" she asked again. "You are far too nice. At any rate you know the reason for those tomfool bag-covers. 'Twas to deaden the smell of liquor. Your generation of Yorkers does not appreciate them as we did." Then her voice broke into derisive sniggers, as she glided away.

And now upon the strange company fell the bellowing of some faithful passing watchman.

"Midnight's here and fair weather!"

A sleepy cock crowed in a distant Chelsea barn.

The faces of the shades began to blanch and assume the lack-lustre tint of ashes. The lady of the banished portrait touched Patricia as if giving her a last embrace, and her smile at Richard Sheridan was full of good wishes.

"Do you consent to the marriage," she whispered, bending over Jonathan, "or shall we come to-morrow night?"

"I do," he answered hoarsely.

"Then we go in peace," sighed the ghost.

There was a flutter of garments and the lights vanished suddenly. Only the scents of old-time perfumes remained, sweet as the hearts of vanished roses.

A cackle of feeble laughter floated back to the room as if the departing Knickerbockers were still making merry on the stairway to the other world.

The song of the weary bells was over. Peace had fallen upon the earth, and in Lady Tyron's mouldering parlor the vials of a foolish pride were despoiled forever. Through the mystical light the living of the family seemed to be strangely transfigured. Jonathan Knickerbocker, the autocrat of York, walked with his head bowed upon his breast. The hard lineaments of Georgina's face were softened. Ofttimes she turned uneasily, half expecting some awful apparition to emerge before her. As for Miss Julie, she moved like one in a dreamland of her own. The tears of the night had fallen upon that little flower in her heart and brought it back to life. Henceforth it would fill all her remaining years with fragrance. The three eldest Knickerbocker daughters clung to her as if she were the guiding light of their starved souls.

Suddenly she left them, and went to her brother.

"I am glad they came, Jonathan," she faltered; "we had forgotten God made us all in His own image. He gave us the flowers and the stars, the sweet winds and the spring-times—the voices of children and the songs of birds. Every man is rich if he but knew it, and those who are only rich in pride are the poorest of the race."

Over by the shimmering casement, the youth and the girl crept nearer to each other. Softly he drew her to him until her face was close to his. The night was dead. Down old Broadway, over the Bowling Green, the Easter dawn tiptoed into the silent city.

CPSIA information can be obtained
at www.ICGtesting.com
Printed in the USA
LVHW041914090222
710699LV00008B/241

9 789355 893895